ANN MORRIS

TOOLS

PHOTOGRAPHS BY
KEN HEYMAN

LOTHROP, LEE & SHEPARD BOOKS

NEW YORK

First Edition   1   2   3   4   5   6   7   8   9   10

Library of Congress Cataloging in Publication Data
Morris, Ann, Tools / by Ann Morris ; photographs by Ken Heyman.
p.   cm.   Summary: Photographs and simple text introduce different devices that we use to make our lives and work
easier.   ISBN 0-688-10170-4. — ISBN 0-688-10171-2 (lib. bdg.)   1. Tools—Juvenile literature.   [1. Tools.   2. Implements,
utensils, etc.]   I. Heyman, Ken, ill.   II. Title.   TJ1195.M73   1992   621.9—dc20   92-3871   CIP   AC

TOOLS

All over the world people use tools.

Tools help us in many ways.

They help us to cut

and pound

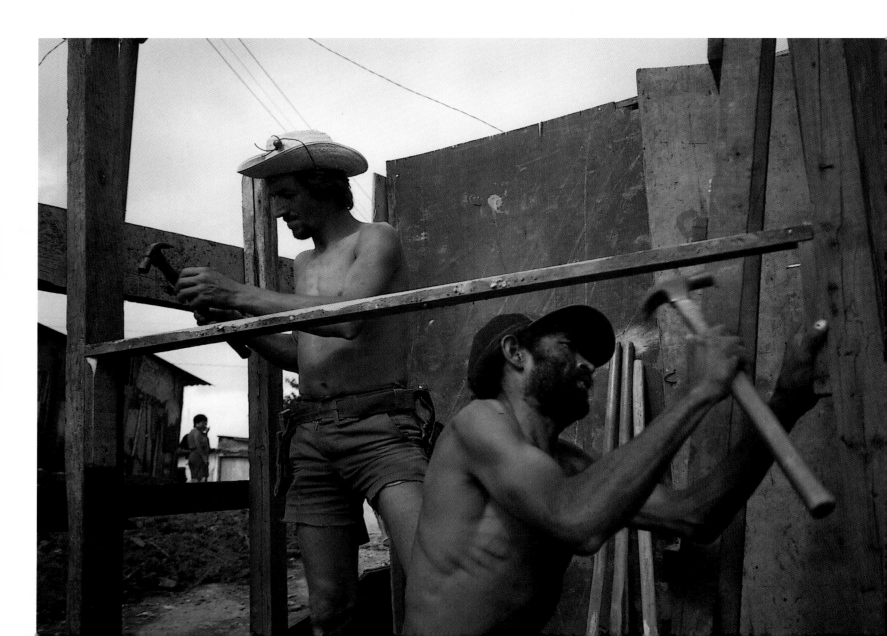

and dig.

We farm with tools.

We cook with tools.

CUSENIER ORANGE

pour mieux
parfumer
et flambe
vos
crêpes

15

We even eat with tools!

16

People use tools to make things

19

and to fix things

and to clean.

23

Tools help us to write

and count

and draw and paint.

Tools help us with our work.

They make our lives easier!

INDEX

16 – 17 UNITED STATES: We use many tools to eat without getting food all over our hands. A spoon works best for ice cream...

and a pair of chopsticks is perfect for picking up bite-sized morsels...

but drinking milk through a straw is just plain fun!

18 UNITED STATES: A Navajo jeweler uses needle-nosed pliers to squeeze silver into a setting that will hold a turquoise stone on the bracelet he has designed.

19 ITALY: This grandmother loops yarn around her neck to keep it untangled as she knits it into clothing with long bone knitting needles.

19 UNITED STATES: A wooden mallet and sharp awl are used to punch perfect, round holes through the leather this young man is crafting into a fine handbag.

20 PERU: This shoemaker uses long tweezers to help him repair a pair of sandals made from old tires.

21 EL SALVADOR: A special blunt needle called a marlinespike is used for making and mending fishing nets.

22 PORTUGAL: This street cleaner uses a stiff brush made of twigs, a shovel, and a stick to clean these cobblestone streets.

23 HAITI: This woman sweeps the pavement in front of her house with a broom so people won't track dirt from the street into her clean home.

24 INDIA: In this school, children use homemade pens and wooden slates instead of pencils and paper. After class the slates are whitewashed so they can be used again the next day.

25 RUSSIA: An abacus is a counting tool that is used in many parts of the world. These children can add and subtract very quickly with this handy tool.

26 CHINA: Drawing with ink requires a delicate brush and a very steady hand.

26 EL SALVADOR: This boy works carefully to paint a flower.

27 MEXICO: A big, square brush is just right for painting a large area quickly.

29 UNITED STATES: The claw end of a hammer is used to pull nails out of wood.

Where in the world were these photographs taken?

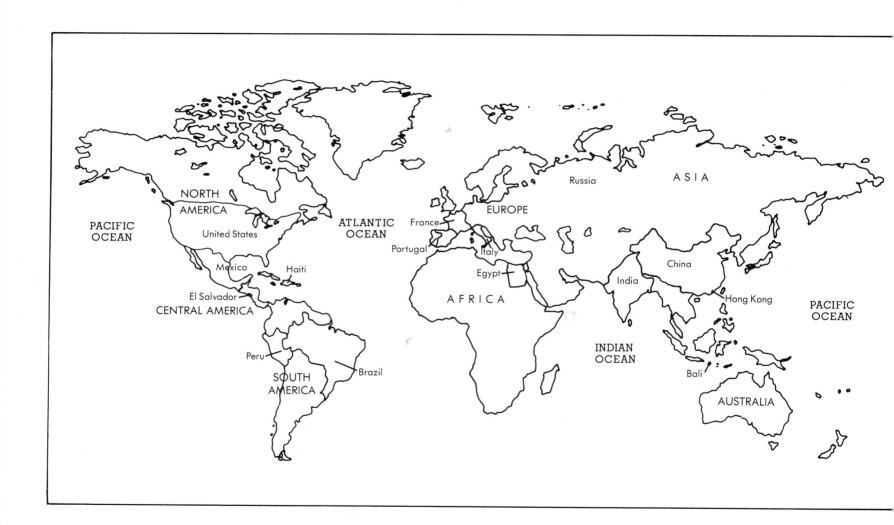